My Life in Water

A Memoir in Essays

by

Cat Pleska

UnCollected Press

My Life In Water
Copyright © 2024 by Cat Pleska

All rights reserved. This book in full or partial form may not be used or reproduced by electronic or mechanical means without permission in writing from the author and UnCollected Press.

Cover Art: Andrea Sinclair and Katie Pleska

Back Cover Portrait: Dan Pleska

Book Design by:

Henry Stanton
UnCollected Press
8320 Main Street, 2nd Floor
Ellicott City, MD 21043

For more books by UnCollected Press:
www.therawartreview.com

First Edition 2024
ISBN: 979-8-9905585-3-3

Table of Contents

Wash Me Clean 1
Strangling Angel 5
Sweet Summer Rain 9
Swimming Lessons 12
Where Fish Dream 16
Narcissus 24
Rising Tide 27
The House on the Hill 32
Water, Water Everywhere 36
One Day on the Lake 38
Take Me Down to the River 45
Videy (Viðey) Island 52
Tossing Jim from the Bridge 66
Water Sign 79
Submersion 83
Water Dreams 87
Washed Clean 91
Angels Float on High 93
Grandfather's Mug 96
Confluence 97
Realization 99

Dedication

I dedicate this book to my husband, Dan, who has sailed with me upon smooth and rough waters, for 50 years.

Wash Me Clean

Norma sat the baby in a claw foot tub of warm water. Norma loved babies and a chance to babysit her little niece made her feel important. She smiled to watch as chubby hands splashed the water's surface. Norma soaped a wash rag and washed the baby's belly then moved to her back. She lifted one splashing hand, and then the other, to massage suds around the fingers. She grabbed the slippery baby and stood her up, scrubbed her bottom and her legs then sat her back down. Rinsing the soap from the rag, she wrung the water out and scrubbed the baby's face, neck, and ears. Norma smoothed the rag over the baby's head, scruffing up wispy hair tufts. Nearly bald when she was born, now, six months later, there was some "peach fuzz" as Norma called it. Her sister, Jean, pretended insult. "My baby does *so* have hair!"

Norma clicked her tongue and said, "I forgot your towel. I'll be right back." She left the baby, newly able to sit, and stepped into the hall to the linen closet. She rummaged for the softest towel, in the meager stack. Her sister didn't have much of anything. She came into the marriage with the clothes on her back. In the year and half since, not much was added, save her child. Norma grabbed a towel and closed the closet door.

She came around the bathroom doorway and a jolt roiled through her body at the sight—no baby in the tub. She dropped the towel and hurried closer. There, completely underwater, lay the baby, staring wide-eyed up at the ceiling. No bubbles, no movement.

Norma reached in and brought her up from under the water. She peered at her face then shook her, gently. "Breathe! Breathe!" She begged.

The baby coughed a little water. She blinked and the wails began. Norma grabbed the towel, brought her fully out of the tub, wrapped her up, and pulled her close. "Shhhh. Shhhh. You're okay. You're all right." The baby calmed to little sobs and then Norma noticed blinking, sleepy eyes. Looking for signs of steady breathing, if she was blue, Norma was relieved she seemed fine.

She dried the baby and took her into the bedroom where she diapered her and dressed her in a sleeper then put her in her crib. The baby kicked a little then stilled, eyes closing. The baby smiled in her sleep, which means she was listening to angels.

Walking to the living room, Norma muttered, "Oh my God! Jean will kill me! What do I know about babies? I'm just 17. She seems okay. She's stopped crying. She's asleep. Jean will never forgive me."

Norma sat down on the couch and put her head in her hands. She resolved: "Well, I just won't tell her." She got up and went into the kitchen. Grabbing the metal coffee pot, she filled it with water, dumped coffee in the metal basket, and pressed on the lid. Setting it on the stove, she searched in the sink drawer for a match. She turned the knob to the stove's burner where she'd placed the pot, lit the match, and the flame caught.

She stared out the window noting the neighbors' houses. She had no phone. Which one would she run to if the baby had not breathed? How do you call the police, or an ambulance, she wondered.

Sipping the strong coffee from her mug, she swallowed hard, and said aloud: "She'll never know."

♦

Decades later, I was visiting Norma, then 84, for Christmas. I had come to dread the eight-hour drive to see her, but I did because Norma's care for me was the closest thing I had to parental attention for a long time. I felt the same way toward her—I would forgive her anything.

One day, on my visit, Norma and I were talking. I don't remember about what, but she turned to me and said, "I nearly drowned you when you were a baby."

Startled, I finally managed to say, "Mom never told me about any of this."

"No, she didn't. She never knew. Here's exactly what happened. What I did."

As I listened, my hand crept up to my neck, and then cradled my chin. I felt adrift. Yet, I knew it was merely an accident, and I could not imagine the anxiety Norma must have felt in not telling my mom for decades.

I also realized before I'd had a chance to say my first words, before my first step, water nearly claimed me.

Strangling Angel

Two women are bathed in the amber light of a single lamp over the kitchen sink. The younger woman sits in an oak chair, a one-year-old baby cuddled to her chest. The older woman stands close, reaching out over and over to place her hand on the baby's forehead. The baby has a fever and her eyes are glazed, staring at something in the middle distance or nothing at all.

"The skin around her mouth . . ." says the grandmother, as she places her hand on the baby's head once again . . . "it's a bit blue. I can't tell in this light." The mother holds the baby under the dim lamp bulb. Neither says anything while they listen to the rattle in the baby's chest as she struggles to pull a breath. The grandmother puts her index finger against the baby's hand. But its fingers do not close around her finger.

"That does it!" The grandmother, suddenly energized, leaves the kitchen, strides through the TV room, through the front bedroom to the living room where the telephone sat on an end table next to the couch. She picks up the receiver and listens. Good. No one is on the party line. It's only 6 p.m. and Geraldine could well have been on there talking to her sister Genevieve, but she must be making dinner. As likely, Mildred was usually on the party line near that hour, debriefing her daughter-in-law on the day's activities. It had snowed all day and probably nothing to report. Grateful she didn't have to ask anyone to get off the line, she dials her doctor's number. When he answers, she explains the baby is sick with fever, she has turned blue, and her breaths are shallow and her chest rattles.

"Well, sounds like the membrane croup or the Strangling Angel . . . that's diphtheria. You should get her to the hospital," the doctor says.

"I can't," the grandmother says. "Warren is stuck at work with the truck. I have no way out. I'm not sure I could even drive out of the holler the snow is so deep. You need to come here."

"I can't get *up* the holler with this snow. You'll have to try to get her out in the morning. Most likely, she'll be dead by then."

"What? You can't do anything? Send an ambulance?"

"No. Not likely they can get up there. I heard the ambulance is out on a car wreck. Try some steam. Maybe it'll help. I'm sorry." He hangs up.

Incredulous, the grandmother stands in the low light of a living room lamp, staring at the silent receiver. She hears just a snippet of someone starting to dial. She slams the phone receiver down.

Striding back to the kitchen, she shouts at the young mother. "Give me that baby! I'll open her up!" Startled, the mother hoists the baby to her, but instead, the grandmother turns and hurries to her kitchen buffet, opens a door, and pulls out a large cast iron skillet. She goes to the stove and bangs the skillet down on a burner, turning it on, waiting a second till the gas flame flares. She dribbles a bit of oil from a silver pot on the stove. Then she rummages in a small bin by the refrigerator and plucks a large onion. In the utensil drawer, she pulls out her favorite paring knife. She peels, washes and cuts up the onion in chunks, dropping them in the hot skillet, stirring with a wooden spoon, turning, turning, letting the chunks soften. As they simmer, she turns to go into the bathroom, rummaging for cheesecloth and finds it in the cabinet under the sink. Yes, enough.

Returning to the stove, she let the onions soften a bit more. She says to the mother, "Take her into the TV room; strip her down to her diaper. Put her on your lap with her feet turned toward the fire." The young mother rises, clutching the baby to her and does as she is told.

When the grandmother deems the onions ready, she places the cheesecloth, doubling, tripling its folds so it would not burn the baby and places a large pile of onion in the middle. She picks the cloth up by its edges and carries it into the TV room where the mother and baby wait.

Gently, the grandmother places the cloth on the baby's pale chest. The baby does not protest, does not move. Her breaths are shallow like a puppy's. The mother cries softly and rubs the baby's feet to warm them against the heat radiating from the small open gas stove.

The baby coughs. Lightly, with a struggle. Then again, again, again. Finally, the coughs grow a little deeper and it becomes clear the pungent onion is working its magic on the tiny body, on the lungs, causing the terrible thick mucus to move. With each cough, the membrane loses its hold, its grip on the little girl's life.

Then they see the blue fade from around the baby's mouth. Her skin, all over, returns to pink. Her toes begin to wiggle. Her eyes focus a bit more. Then she turns her head to look directly at her grandmother.

♦

My mother sobs in relief. My grandmother reaches out her hand, putting her index finger against the palm of mine. I grasp it firmly. I pull warmth and strength from my grandmother on the night I was predicted to die.

Sweet Summer Rain

Built on the walls of a cinder block cellar, above spider webs, jars of pole beans, crocks of pickled corn and baskets of russet potatoes, was the cellar house, a small 15 by 10 foot room. It stood up the hill a few dozen feet behind my grandparents' house.

Tin roofed and painted white, its trim buttercup yellow, the small room had two windows. It also had two doors, but one opened to air because the thirteen silvery wooden steps had been removed when the wood grew rotten. But it was after my mother had once fallen down those stairs. As she tumbled from top to bottom, her grip on me loosened, and my two-year-old body sailed through the air. I landed on my head, suffering a bump behind my ear.

As I grew older, but still a child, I often sought the solitude and comfort of the cellar house. My family used it for storage, but over the years different family members had stayed in it. Whenever I went up there, I'd dig down in an old hump-backed trunk full of *Mutt and Jeff* comic books, past scraps of quilting fabric, to my dad's army uniform at the bottom. Along with the uniform, was a dark woolen quilt I needed to snuggle under. It had been sewn by my great grandmother. She had cut, pieced, and quilted material she had saved from old suits and overcoats, building a durable cover to last several lifetimes.

The only furniture in the cellar house was an old, white iron bedstead. It was three-quarter size and had belonged to my great-grandparents. Atop the bed was a feather tick mattress of blue ticking and stuffed with duck feathers and down.

Plucking the wool quilt from the trunk, I'd run and plunge into the tick puffed high on the iron bed like a loaf of yeast bread ready to go in the oven. I'd sink into the mattress and be startled for a few seconds, thinking there was no bottom. Falling down into the dark and quiet, I'd pull the scratchy quilt over myself like a monk needing a hair shirt, and I'd hope for a rowdy thunderstorm. Some days, my hopes came true.

First, the wind would come up and trees would moan and whisper in response. Faintly at first, I would hear the thunder rumble. Then the thunder's timbre deepened and boomed and rattled the glass in the windows. Lightning flashed so bright I could see it through my closed eyelids. From my safe place, swaddled in ticking and wool, I let the fear take over.

Rain would begin its hesitant patter then build with the wind to a solid crescendo. Deeper I'd sink into the tick, drifting down to where no one and nothing but me belonged. Then the wind would calm, and the rain would settle down to its most serious business. It would echo and drum with such an intensity I thought it would surely pound through the tin roof, sluice through wool and flesh and bone, bearing traces of me on through tick and iron and wood—splash down to the cellar below, to webs and beans and potatoes and nasty pickled corn, and then dribble onto the concrete floor. Then it'd seep out through the walls at the base of the cellar, into the dark, rich soil. It'd flow by the earthworms and grubs and moles, down to the water table and into the well. It'd get drawn up in a tin bucket, cold and pure as melted glacier ice, and they would drink me in.

I'd lie still for the whole time it rained, from first splatters on the roof, to torrent, to the steady drip from the eaves to silence. And in the stillness, I'd throw back the quilt and rub the blotches on my bare legs and arms from the scratchy wool.

I'd clamber out of the tick, throw open the door, and inhale the ozone. I listened and then heard the faint cries of the tree frog peepers in the rain-swollen creek. They'd chorus louder and louder.

Calling for someone to love them.

Swimming Lessons

My mother didn't drive, so if I went anywhere in our small town, nestled at the confluence of the Ohio and Kanawha Rivers, it was with friends whose mothers drove. One friend and I agreed, at ten years old, we needed to learn to swim; that way, we could beg to be taken to the swimming pool. So far, it was already hot for early June. It would be heaven to swim all summer and have no chaperone.

I was at her house when her mother finally agreed. I was surprised because Maria was in one of her bad moods. She slipped into them from time to time, I overheard my mother say. She would cuss and complain, compulsively remove any knickknacks from her house, even take up the colorful rugs, as if it all offended her eyes.

Citing bible verses about vanity, to no one in particular, she also dressed in monk brown and nun black. She stood, arms crossed, staring out at the infernal world in cold silence, not cooking for her family or cleaning the now bare house. If she were angry at my friend, I saw her jerk her by her arm, insisting she obey, yelling and then falling over, exhausted.

These times of silence and anger coincided with her husband disappearing after work. Where he went, I didn't know and my friend never said. She didn't talk about her mother's moods, either, except to say, "My mother is such an idiot." I startled to hear her say this. It never occurred to me to complain about my mom in such a way. I didn't understand, but I also didn't ask. I viewed my friend as braver and more assured than I was. She scared me a little, but she was the only girl near my age in my neighborhood, and mostly we had fun.

Swimming lessons were scheduled at the city pool to start the next week, on a Monday. That morning, I got up and changed into my bathing suit, grabbed a towel from the linen closet and waited outside our house on the front lawn for my friend and her mom to pick me up. Once at the pool, Maria would leave, promising to come back for us at the end of the lesson.

An older man, the teacher, talked to us about safety: what to do in case of sinking; how to tread water; how to signal when you're in trouble.

Finally, we slipped into the frigid pool water. We were in the shallow end and the teacher stood poolside and instructed the class how to float, how to put your face in the water, pulling your head up just enough to breathe then put it in the water again.

As the week progressed, we stepped further into the pool toward the deep end. We practiced strokes, keeping our fingers tightly together, floating on our backs and practicing the back stroke.

On Friday, we advanced to the deep end, ten feet of water, to perform our final test. All we had to do was push away from the side of the pool and then swim back. My friend went before me. I watched as she hung onto the pool's side. Then she pushed and glided out to the middle of the pool. She floated a few seconds then I watched her sink. She didn't flail as she sank further down to the bottom. I looked at our teacher as he watched her. Then he seemed to come out of a daze, bent at the waist, ready to dive in. But my friend waved her arms at her sides, kicked her feet, and rose, but her head didn't pop above the surface. She had kicked closer to the pool's side so the teacher reached down, grabbed her arm, and pulled her up. Her grip on his arm was so tight he had to pry her off as she plopped down at poolside. She strangled-coughed. Water poured from her mouth, her nose, her long black hair streamed over her face. She flopped onto her back, coughing. After a moment, when she quieted, the teacher, satisfied she was okay, turned to speak to us. I asked my friend if she was all right. She silently nodded.

Afterwards, I refused to jump in the deep end, so I never earned my swimming certificate.

I don't remember if she told her mother what happened or if she ever learned to swim. But two days later, Maria left for an institution where they treated the mentally ill, my mother told me. "It used to be called the Trans Allegheny Lunatic Asylum," my mother said to my dad, explaining what had happened, again.

In the vague way children listen to adults talk, apparently Maria had been there before and stayed for several weeks each time. When she returned, everything was right as rain. She was cheerful, visiting friends. The knickknacks returned as did the colorful rugs. She wore bright house dresses. My favorite was robin's egg blue.

My friend said, "She'll go back there again. She always does." She snorted, shaking her head.

When I was sixteen, after I had moved away, word came Maria had returned to the institution again. This time, she did not return. Another patient had pushed her into one of the ponds on the grounds. She drowned.

I never learned to swim. I had recurrent nightmares about drowning. I thought I must have drowned in a previous lifetime, unlike Maria who swallowed unending bitterness and despair, who might have found the pond a release.

Where Fish Dream

A bitter wind pummeled me as I stood at the river's edge in Point Pleasant, West Virginia. A bright sun is rendered useless when temperatures are near freezing. It had been cold but clear on a dark night long ago, and I wondered if icy temperatures had been a blessing when 46 people fell to the bottom of the river and died. Did the shock of the frigid water help numb them so they wouldn't feel the weight of hundreds of thousands of pounds of bridge steel push them down into the soft river bottom?

That sunny, freezing day, as I stood by the Ohio River and studied the stumps of bridge supports, I imagined drivers' and passengers' shock when they felt the shaky bridge wobble up and down more than usual. Did they clutch their chests, grab one another's hands? Did they lunge forward to grab the dash as the car nosed down or did the suddenness of the fall lift them from their seats for a moment? How long did it take for them to fade to blackness?

Did any of them understand what was happening to them on December 15, 1967, the day the Silver Bridge fell?

♦

My family and I had moved to the river town of Point Pleasant when I was four because my dad took a job at Ravenswood Aluminum in a nearby town. Many times my Aunt Norma would drive from her home a half hour away and pick up my mother, who did not drive, to travel across the Ohio River to shop. I remember sitting in the back seat of my aunt's car when we drove across the river. I remember the shaking of the Silver Bridge, but the town's leaders had said: It is the way of suspension bridges. They will shimmy a bit; it is safe.

Until it wasn't.

◆

When I was in the 7th grade, I came home from school one day to find my mother and my aunt waiting for me. "Pack your suitcase," my mother directed. "Take only a few toys. We'll come for them and the rest of your clothes another time." My mother had reached a point of no return with my father, who'd been drunk and practically living in beer joints for days, drowning in beer and whisky. She had lied to his foreman one last time that he was sick and could not come to work. She refused to make excuses for him any longer, not for work, not for herself.

I was thrust mid-year into a new junior high school in another town, bumbling around trying to find rooms and friends. I shook all that first day, terrified. Why did you come here, some asked. I lied and said my dad had moved to this town for a new job. My mother and I moved into my aunt's house. We shared one bedroom. My few belongings I'd managed to bring with me took up one drawer in a dresser. My mother did not have much more.

A few weeks later, when we returned to our home in Point Pleasant to gather more clothes and other items, we discovered my father had hired a junk man to come take all our belongings away. Everything was gone. We had no warning. I leaned against my bedroom wall, trying to comprehend, sliding down to the floor. I collapsed into a heap, sobbing. I didn't own much, but what little I had was thrown away by my dad.

My mother cried and cried. She ran out of tissues and used her sleeve to wipe her eyes and nose as we drove back to my aunt's house in silence. I was bewildered and did not understand much of anything that was happening. I only knew my life was forever changed.

♦

At first, the news reported thirty-six people had died in the bridge collapse. A later counting raised the number to forty-six. Families, lone drivers, commercial truck drivers, men, women, and children, all perished in a horrific way ten days before Christmas. Rumors sprang up immediately, saying it was the curse of Mothman or the two-hundred-year-old curse of the Native American Cornstalk had caused the collapse. The people on both sides of the Ohio River asked: how did this *really* happen? It would be four years before they would discover the supporting eye-bar 330 had failed, causing the bridge to collapse on that cold night with the crystal sky. The bridge had been constructed with little redundancy; if one part failed, nothing would keep the rest of the structure from failing too (Meigsindypress.com).

When the bridge was completed in 1928, it was designed for Model T cars weighing 1,500 pounds and commercial vehicles of 20,000 pounds. At the time of its collapse, cars weighed 4,000 pounds and commercial trucks weighed around 60,000 pounds. With such overloads, failure was predictable. Bridges, and people, can only stand so much weight.

From the beginning, the builders cut corners. The bridge was originally meant to be suspended with traditional wire cables. However, an alternate bid for an eye-bar design ended up being cheaper. Plus, this design would make the bridge one of the first structures of its kind in the United States, something the town fathers in West Virginia and Ohio could brag about. The eye-bars were vital for the structural integrity of the bridge, yet there was no way to thoroughly inspect them without taking the bridge apart. So, no one knew an eye-bar had become defective until it was too late.

♦

My mother, as a naïve eighteen-year-old, met my father one day walking to the dime store where she worked. She was enchanted with my father's movie star looks and swagger. They courted a few months then were married on a cold January day. Photographs taken of my mother earlier on the day of her wedding showed her somber face. Doubt radiated from her even in a black and white image. It was as if she knew something was wrong. In truth, however, she did not know my father was already an alcoholic at twenty-four. At the first of their marriage, all seemed okay, until well into her pregnancy with me later in the first year. When I was older, she told me Dad had been gone for several days. She had no food, save a few potatoes. She had no one to call, even if she had a phone. And no salt for the potatoes cooking on the stove.

With nowhere to go or escape, she and Dad managed to live together for the next several years, until the fateful day when I was twelve and the house of cards fell.

⬥

A loud noise like a gunshot sounded when the bridge began to fall. Witnesses said it "folded like a deck of cards." Divers searched for hours, seeking the people in the cars, to recover them. Down there on the bottom of the river, the divers saw in the murky waters huge shapes floating by, most likely channel catfish, or channel cats as they're called, as long as school buses. They lived down there, sifting through the muck, floating and dreaming in the dark.

⬥

One day, about two months after Mom and I had left Point Pleasant, I was on the couch watching television with my cousin. A knock on the door led Mom to open it and in walked Dad. He was dressed in freshly-pressed beige work shirt and pants. His hair was slicked back with Brylcreem, accenting the natural wave. He smelled of cologne and his black shoes were shiny.

I could never get the whole story, but bits and pieces came to me. My aunt confided when I was grown it was my mother who had asked him to come. My aunt was upset with her saying Mom was fine where she was and didn't need to take Dad back. I suspected living with my aunt and uncle simply wasn't working well for Mom. With no high school diploma, no car, and no money, I'm sure Mom realized: what choice did she have?

One concession Dad agreed to was to move to a town near where my aunt lived, accepting he had a long commute to work. My aunt became my mother's chauffeur to stores, to the doctor, until I got my license and could take her where she needed to go. I don't doubt Mom cried a river of tears for the rest of her life.

♦

On the day of the bridge collapse, two years after my mother and father reunited, my mother and my aunt were on the way to Christmas shop. When they reached Henderson, a small town next to Point Pleasant, cars were backed up for several miles. They sat trapped in motionless traffic until near midnight, not knowing what had happened, until they were finally able to turn around and drive home. On the eleven o'clock news, which continued coverage on the disaster through the night, Mom and my aunt learned of the bridge's collapse and reeled at the thought they, too, might have been on the bridge when it fell.

As the years passed, my mother became weary of my father's drinking and verbal abuse. She spent much of her time in a state of despair, positive nothing would ever be fixed, her marriage permanently flawed. She came to believe she would die before my father, the ultimate unfairness of her life. Perhaps it was a self-fulling prophecy, but she developed lung cancer, and at her life's end, pneumonia overwhelmed her frail body as her lungs filled to beyond capacity.

♦

The newspapers reported the results of testing on the cause of the bridge collapse. "The fracture was caused by the development of a critical-size flaw over the 40-year life of the structure as the result of the joint action of stress corrosion and corrosion fatigue." Further laboratory work concluded: "With the north … chain thus broken, the structure's design made total collapse … inevitable" (meigsindypress.com).

♦

My parents' marriage lasted forty-six years. That night of the bridge collapse forty-four bodies were recovered. Two more, Kathy Byus and Maxine Turner, both of Point Pleasant, were never found.

When someone drowns, it is usually fairly quick. My mother's drowning was her decades-long struggle to cope with my father's behavior. I am convinced the weight of worry crushed her. Maybe when she died there was brief relief in the form of numbness until, finally, there was no more pain.

Narcissus

A small drainage pond sat a few yards behind our green-painted cinderblock house. Construction in the area required a pond to collect the water run-off from the changing landscape. I made a daily trek to stand by the edge and watch the surface.

Becoming a teenager was confusing. I had pimples, body changes, and greasy hair which made me uncomfortable. Mom's depression worsened and she had more days when nothing was funny or fun. She smoked cigarettes, complained to her sister, Norma. The two of them visited yard sales on the weekend, but the rest of time Mom cleaned. It did not seem like fun to be an adult, but I figured I had no choice. I had no way to know what being an adult meant, or anyone to ask. The adults in my life seemed to be as confused as to who they wanted to be as I was.

Dad's drinking had increased, and sometimes he didn't come home. Mom hated lying to his foreman, saying he was sick. When he was home, he worked on his car in the driveway, or messed around with the two beagle pups he had adopted, who he called Mutt and Jeff.

One cool October morning, I eagerly awaited the school bus. Mom had agreed to buy me makeup: bright blue eye shadow and black mascara. I couldn't wait to try them and anticipated what my classmates would say. Finally, I was moving into teenagehood, on my way to adult. I held my head up, greeting every student, but only two people commented: "Good grief! What's wrong with your eyes?" "Oh. Bright enough for ya?"

My face still felt aflame as I got off the bus that afternoon. I dropped my schoolbooks off in the house and headed straight for the pond.

I should have named the pond Beauty Pond, or Serene Pond, or maybe Acceptance Pond. The pond was always there, where bull frogs croaked their deep baritone in the spring. In the summer heat, the pond harbored mosquitoes which fed the bats that swooped at night. White tailed deer, legs splayed, drank from the pond. On stormy days, small white caps flipped up and the water turned gunmetal grey, like the sky.

No fish swam in the pond because no one stocked it, but to me it was alive and on windy days, it lapped against the bank, trickling, and bumping its way back to its original shape. I never saw the bottom, and I wondered what I couldn't see.

I had bought a cheap diary with a small key, and I wrote every day describing what the pond looked like, how the surface changed. I also wrote about boys, how I was smitten with this one or the other. Or what happened at school, or a visit to my grandparents. Each day needed a meditation at the pond's edge.

That sunny afternoon, of the day when I first wore makeup, I got off the bus, near tears. I leaned over the Pond's edge until I could see my face reflected on the surface. I could not see well enough to note my bright blue eye shadow and my darkened, lengthened lashes. I looked the same in the Pond's reflection. Refocusing, no matter the bright day, I still could not see the bottom. Always muddy, always murky. I straightened up from my crouch by the pond in time to see a barn swallow swoop over the water, snatching a gnat as it flew by.

My mother asked me after dinner if I was going to remove my makeup before I went to bed. I said, "No. I'm going to sleep in it." She shrugged, and lit another cigarette, returned to watching television.

Next morning, I went in the bathroom to prepare for my school day. I washed off the makeup and studied my reflection in the mirror. I lightly patted a bare hint of color on my eyelids and used one layer of mascara.

Before the bus came, I stopped by the pond. The light had shifted on the surface leaving it shimmering in the early sun; I wrote in my diary; *Like you, Pond, I am changing, but I cannot yet see what is there deep down. I don't know when things will be clear.*

Rising Tide

The Atlantic! My first time seeing the ocean. I'd traveled there with my aunt, uncle, and a cousin. We were camping and it was a first, too. My cousin, at 16 was two years older than I, said multiple times he couldn't wait to see girls in bathing suits. He bounced around in the backseat until our aunt said, "Be still! You're rocking the car!" He hung his head out the window like a dog, lolling his tongue out, trying to make me laugh, which he usually did.

When we arrived, the campground was a couple blocks back from the beach. After we set up the tent and unloaded groceries, we changed into our bathing suits in the bathhouse. I came out to join my family on the short walk to the beach. My aunt handed me a towel and my cousin carried a small shovel and pail, for sandcastles he said.

I was ten when I read *The Bobbsey Twins at the Seashore.* I'd seen photos and heard friends talk about going to the ocean, about getting sunburned, building castles, and playing in the surf, collecting seashells.

Finally, I got my first sight of the ocean. I stopped. It was . . . immense. Coming from a land-locked state, surrounded by mountains, my vista never changed. My line of sight stopped a short distance away, and my eyes rested up against tree-lined hills. A tremble swept through me, though I was warm from the sun. I had gotten used to my back-yard pond, but this was unfathomable.

My cousin tossed the shovel and pail toward me, and ran full tilt for the water, till he encountered a wave into which he plunged headlong. My aunt and uncle seemed not to notice as they looked for a smooth, flat surface to put down their towels. I placed mine beside theirs and walked toward the surf. I stopped short. I dropped down on my haunches, rocked back on my butt, with my arms wrapped around my knees. I stared at the endless body of water filling my sight.

I could hear my cousin's joyful screams as he dove into wave after wave. My aunt had plopped down on her towel and brought a bottle of baby oil out of her beach bag. She began to slather on the oil and when finished, lay back to bake in the sun. My uncle came to stand beside me. "Going in?" He asked.

"Not just yet. I want to sit here a minute." I didn't want him to see I was scared.

He walked toward the ocean then dived into the waves just as my cousin had.

The ocean breeze stiffened my hair with salt and eventually the spray coated my glasses blurring my view. I took them off and carried them back to my towel. It was time to step into the water.

Unlike my cousin and my uncle, my steps into the sea were hesitant, playing at the edge of the surf, allowing my skin to be exposed to the cold seawater gradually. I inhaled the strong smell—salt water and something else, I couldn't identify what exactly—earthy maybe? Something . . . fishy? Well, of course, I thought. But I had never been near the sea.

I was in up to my waist, and I began to float up and down with the swells. My uncle was farther out and I could barely make out my cousin's head just above the waves. Without my glasses all was blurred, and the sun glinting off the surface water made seeing even more difficult. I looked toward the shore, for my aunt, but I couldn't see her.

My uncle called to me to come out to him. I shook my head no. I did not know if I could keep my head above the higher waves, and I could see well enough to know they were rising over my uncle's head. He rode up and down on the big waves. Then he made his way to where I was and held out his hand. "Come on. I'll show you how to keep your head above water. You don't need to know how to swim."

I stared for a few seconds at his out-stretched hand. He was the same age as my father, but I could not imagine in a million years my dad reaching his hand out to me. I'd never even kissed his cheek. We were both in the same house, but I was never in his thoughts, drunk or sober.

I took his hand, noting the strangeness, and we walked farther out, letting our bodies be lifted up and back down. Finally, he turned and looked back at the beach and told me to do so also. As I turned, I noticed a large wave headed for us, clearly over my head. I panicked, but my uncle hung on to my hand as the wave broke, pouring what felt like a huge bucket of cold water over me. As it moved on to shore, I stood in water up to my neck, sputtering and coughing, rubbing burning sea water out of my eyes. Then I heard my uncle warn, "Here comes another!"

This time, he grabbed my hand more firmly and pulled it up, and the rest of me with it. My head stayed above the wave. He then pulled me a little closer to shore in chest deep water, and we held hands, letting the ocean lift us up and gently set us back down.

After what seemed like hundreds of lifts and falls, my uncle said, "Come on. Let's go back in. I'm hungry. You?" I nodded. The sun had turned his back red. He was solid, like a big rock forcing the waves to go around.

He let go my hand and I walked back toward the beach, stopping for a few minutes where the water came to my waist, feeling the swells rise and fall; it felt like a kiddy carnival ride. My father's image flitted through my mind. A few years before, when he had learned I failed to pass the swimming test, he shook his head. "Well, if you don't learn, you'll drown someday. Need to learn." He turned back to his newspaper.

The next day, I rose early before my family, and left them sleeping. I dressed in the bath house. I wanted to walk on the beach by myself. I found small shells and collected several. The ocean seemed quieter, as if it hadn't wakened yet. As the sun climbed, it shone out across the water and sparkled in yellows and oranges in a path straight toward me. I clutched my seashells to my chest and watched as the land let loose of the sun. Remembering a book of geography we read in school, I knew water covers three fourths of our planet, and once all the continents were gathered in one large land mass. Over time, many of the huge hunks of land drifted apart. I imagined those pieces of land, straining to touch again.

The House on the Hill

Once there was a house on the hill with two newly married fools in it.

The long and winding driveway was dirt and gravel. Spring rains turned the narrow lane leading up to it to mud and traveling it daily to work and whatnot meant the ruts grew deeper by the day.

One day, the wife fool stepped out of her four-wheel drive truck and into a rut up to her thigh. Granted, she wasn't a tall person, but still. In the winter, snow and ice ensured the driveway was treacherous. More than once, the wife fool and the husband fool felt their vehicle slide backward, out of control, on the ice. They simply slid into a field and were okay. Fortunately, sometimes the gods do you a favor, though you are a fool.

The driveway had no place to dig ditches on either side to carry water away because the whole road was built on massive rock. The expensive gravel they had dumped on the drive to gain purchase when they drove up washed down and into the field when it rained hard. After a couple years of this folly, they hired a company to change the driveway so it traveled along the side of the hill and not straight up. The newly gouged driveway, though longer, had ditches on each side to carry the rainwater away properly so the expensive gravel stayed put.

City water lines were a long, distant dream, in terms of time and money. The only way water came into the house pipes was via a cistern in the ground. This is a holding tank made of cinder block buried close to the house so gutters directed rainwater from the roof to the cistern. For a while, as long as it rained, there was water for showering, washing clothes, boiling to wash the dishes. They drank bottled water from the grocery store, especially after the wife fool checked the cistern and found mating garter snakes floating. With no way out. Fortunately, it was a smaller cistern. They had another, a new one they built, and it was snake proof. They hoped.

The previous house's owner employed a dowser to find water to dig a well. He found water 225 feet down, but there was not enough to bother pumping up to the house.

When it did not rain, the two naïve folks called for a big truck to drive up the long driveway and fill the cistern with city water. In the winter, the roads would be too icy, so they resorted to melting snow. You'd be surprised how much snow it takes to fill a sink to wash dishes.

The sewer was yet another big tank in the ground. But it was okay the two fools were happy to note.

To warm the house, it had an old oil-fired furnace, but it was not easy getting the oil holding tank filled—especially when the roads were impossible to travel on by the oil trucks. Then the old furnace caught fire and could not be used. Fortunately, it did not burn the house down as there would have been no water to put it out. They bought a wood burning stove and connected it to the fireplace to vent up the chimney. One winter, it was so cold, the two gullible folks could not stay warm, no matter how much wood they brought in to feed the stove. So, they left to stay with their parents.

When they returned, the water pipes in the basement were frozen, and twisted like the gnarled fingers of a troll. All the pipes had to be replaced, which the husband fool did himself. Between working and being home, it took him four months. The wife fool joked she could take a bath in a teacup.

After seven years, they sold the house on the hill to another family. The two weary fools moved to a flat lot, a brand new house, in another town. Everything worked, water was abundant, sewer from the house flowed over on the other side of the town and not in a buried tank in the yard; it was warm in the winter and there was no mud, no ditches, just occasional ice, like everywhere else.

The two fools learned their lesson. They were not cut of the mold of some folks to cope, endure, and do without water. They were no pioneers; they were not back-to-the-landers, like they wanted to be. They were softer.

The only thing they missed from the house on the hill was the spectacular view from the front yard. The windows spread across the expanse of the front of the house and their eyes lifted to see row upon row of hills falling away into the mist, like ocean waves of earth.

Water, Water Everywhere

The car phone rang. I noted the number: a friend in our neighborhood. Why would he be calling us? We were traveling back from a vacation at the beach. What could be so urgent?

My husband, Dan, answered the phone and I could hear the voice on the other end: our house had been flooded. Several houses in our subdivision were also flooded when the creek which skirted our homes overflowed with the Flood of the Century, they called it.

Exceeding the speed limit whenever Dan thought he could get away with it, we flew home.

We lived in a mid-entry—a house style that when you entered it you went upstairs to the main living quarters or downstairs where there were more bedrooms, my office, and a family room. Now, with 8-10 inches of water standing in the lower half of the house.

One of the neighbors had called a locksmith and broke into our house. Then several friends entered to move what they could to safety, to the dry floor upstairs. But much was lost: carpeting, furniture, our daughter's toys on the floor, books on the bottom shelves of bookcases, closets where photos were stored—now ruined.

It was July and we had to move fast as the heat would ensure mold would begin to grow. For weeks we both toiled whenever we could. The carpet and drywall were removed, and the sodden household goods taken to the dump. Our insurance paid for the repairs, which Dan elected to do himself. But it was almost too much for him. We replaced walls and painted; ordered new carpet and bought furniture. But finally, it was completed and back to some sense of normal.

Until the next year, when within days of the other Flood of the Century's anniversary, another deluge came.

This time, Dan almost didn't cope with the water loss, the damage. But it meant money in the bank to undertake the damage repair ourselves. To a young family, the money gained meant a better life enjoyed. He did most of it, again. I helped wherever I could, whenever I could. It almost wasn't enough, but Dan made it through and put the house together again. I was proud of his hard work. A few years later, we moved once again, to a house on a smaller hill than before, a knoll, really. Only once in a great while, during torrential downpours, does the basement of this house gain a little water. So far, no inundation.

One Day on the Lake

I heard it was a serene day. A good day for boating. I heard a storm rose, without warning, as June storms can do.

Five in the boat. The two men and the young boy fished. Bluegill and sunfish may not have been biting. The heat would drive the fish lower, away from the too bright sun and then the storm loomed. The women were surely bored anyway, and getting too hot, burnt from the sun.

Realizing the lake was no place to be in a storm, they sped to the shoreline of an island in the lake. The clouds covered the sky, shades of grey and almost black. They hovered close to the five boaters. Others on the lake said it was a smothering feeling.

As they drove the boat to a shallow cove, they stepped out of the water up to their ankles as thunder rumbled. A cool wind swept through as they stepped on land and stopped near trees. Friends thought maybe they knew the tree could draw lightning, so they wouldn't have stood directly under one, but the island they had come to was covered with trees. Then the strike came, hit the tree closest to the five. The million-degree bolt raged down the branches, through the trunk and into the roots—even the ones exposed above ground. The roots the five were standing on, beside the lake.

I saw the article in the *New York Times*, a fluke I even saw it. It was rare I had the chance or the time to read the *Times*. Maybe it was the article title which caught my eye. It said, "Five Killed by Lightning." I thought later the reason it was in the *Times* was because the younger man, Harrison, had been in the Marines and assigned to the White House when Reagan was in office. Otherwise, a family, no matter it was all five, from West Virginia would not make any kind of news. But there it was: the story of this family for the world to read. I did not find it in any state newspapers, perhaps a local one, near Lake Moomaw.

So I knew I'd have to tell my dad, who I was sure did not know about it yet.

Mom answered the phone. "Mom, Harrison, Matthew, Sheila and her aunt and uncle were struck by lightning on Lake Moomaw. All of them were standing on tree roots. It killed all five of them."

"Hmmm." Mom said. Then "How'd you find out?"

"It was in the *New York Times*. I just happened to be reading the latest issue." Silence. Then "Do you want me to tell Dad?"

"I guess you should." She called Dad to the phone.

"Dad, Harrison and his family, including his wife's aunt and uncle were up on Lake Moomaw. They got out of the boat when a storm came up, but lightning hit a tree they were near and the lightning went through the roots. It killed all five of them."

"Huh, well, I'll be damned."

Silence. Then …

"I guess I better call Zeph." Zeph was Harrison's father and my dad's mountain friend.

"Yeah, I guess so."

"Okay, well thanks for calling."

"Okay. Bye."

◆

Once, I went to visit my parents, well before Harrison and family were killed. I found Mom in the kitchen cooking dinner. Dad was at the end of the table with the newspaper open.

"I left my shotgun with Harrison, the one my grandfather gave me," Dad was saying. He didn't look up at Mom to see if she was listening. "He wanted to practice cross hatching on the stock." Dad chuckled. "I told him he was welcome to try." Dad chuckled again. He chuckled a lot when he was in a good mood and sober.

Mom grunted and continued cooking.

"He seemed tickled when I asked him to work with my gun. Next time I'm up in the mountains, Harrison said he'd have my gun ready."

Mom stirred the gravy, saying nothing.

♦

Another time, I came to visit my parents just as Dad was coming out of the house, toting a duffle bag and his fishing rod.

"Where are you going, Dad?"

"Up in the mountains, Lake Moomaw. I promised Harrison I'd go with him and Matthew."

How old is Matthew now?" I'd never met any of them.

"He's about eight."

♦

Christmas came, I remember, in the months before the family died. Mom was wrapping gifts. I saw a box with a toboggan in it.

"Mom, did you buy this toboggan hat for Katie? She doesn't wear toboggans." Katie is my daughter, her only grandchild.

Mom grabbed the box with the hat in it. "No, it's for Matthew. Your dad picked it out himself. I don't recall he *ever* picked out a present for you. I always did it." She measured out Christmas paper for the box and began wrapping it, saying nothing more.

♦

My dad was pretty broken up over the death of Harrison and his family, but he and Zeph held it together pretty well, others at the funeral reported. Mom didn't go. When I asked her why not, she said, "They were not my family. Not your family. You are his only child, and he seemed to care about Harrison more than he did you." I said nothing about this, but Mom was silent for a moment then said, "I can't begin to know how a whole family must feel losing all of them . . . as well as your dad . . . ." She left the obvious unsaid.

I measured how I felt about this. I never thought about how much he cared for Harrison, a few years older than me. In fact, in thinking about it in the face of such a massive loss, I realized I'd always thought he regarded Harrison as the son he never had. Mom had told me years ago when she was pregnant with me, Dad said he hoped it was a boy. Mom hoped just as fervently it was not. She did not want a carbon copy of her husband, the man who drank and kept her life in turmoil. She won. But I'm sure she never factored in the possibility another's man's son might be the answer to Dad's longing.

The time was past for me to care he regarded Harrison and Matthew so fondly. For me, it was water under the bridge.

In the years since, both my parents gone, I think of Harrison from time to time. I was sure he never gave Mom or me a thought, but Dad probably said little about either of us. When he was in the mountains, he had a mountain family. Two families. I'm just as sure Harrison regarded my father, an older man who showed him how to hunt and fish, like a beloved uncle. Maybe he felt loved, or at least cared for, by my father. I, on the other hand, had a mother who loved me, and though it might seem odd, it was always enough.

Maybe it was an okay trade-off. Dad never knew how to deal with me, a girl. What do girls do anyway? Play dolls? He didn't know how to.

In my mind, I see Lake Moomaw on that serene day, sun shimmering on the water. A day full of fun and hope. I feel most sorry for young Matthew, who was loved by his family, who had barely just begun. As for all of them, lives cut so short and so unfairly, I can only feel a deep, abiding sorrow.

Maybe what Dad taught Harrison is blood is *not* thicker than water. Maybe it's much more fluid, this who-you-love business. Maybe it flows the path of least resistance if you let it. Maybe you float on this notion of the fluidity of love as being a boat on the lake taking you to more solid ground, where all you can do is hope you are safe.

https://www.nytimes.com/1994/06/20/us/5-killed-by-lightning.html

Take Me Down to the River

My husband's job as a warehouseman with a chemical company put him in contact with suppliers. One of them treated customers to rafting trips on the New River. I was invited to go, too, the first year. Knowing my fear of water, my husband assured me I would be safe. The river guides were experienced, he said, and they'd ride the rapids in the smartest and safest ways.

That first year, we had a female guide whose sense of humor and superb storytelling ability kept us laughing the whole trip. She guided us through the rapids with confidence and with safety in mind. I anticipated the same experience when we were invited to go the second year.

I was once again standing in a group of fellow raters at the river's edge. As the raft guide, a male this time, talked about safety, I shifted uneasily in the large life vest strapped around my chest. After the safety speech, we climbed aboard the rafts, took up our paddles and we were soon floating downstream.

Rapids are rated from one to five, depending on their severity. The first set of rapids we paddled thorough felt like going over the ridges of an old fashioned washboard. Exhilarating and fun. I paddled when he told my side of the raft to do so and listened to his instructions, watching as the water began to get rougher. He told us dirty jokes between hollering "Paddle left! Paddle right!" meaning those on the left or right needed to dig in the water with their paddles as fast and as hard as they could. The rapids became lengthier and deeper. I noticed my husband, at the bow of the raft, leaned forward, causing the front of the raft to dip even further below the water line, the better to be splashed, making the ride rougher. We were dressed in shorts and t-shirts, but I was beginning to regret not wearing a bathing suit.

After a series of rapids, none categorized worse than a three, I felt confident I could ride out the rest of the day safely. We all knew the river claimed at least one person a year, though, usually if they were caught in a hydraulic, a place where water drops over a ledge or big rock, causing deeper water on the downstream side. The water can be drawn back toward the rock or ledge, creating a hole, with a powerful downward pull. If you got caught in one, it is likely you would not get out, nor be saved. We'd been told usually none of the rapids on that stretch of the river were labeled higher than a four. Unless, it hadn't rained, the raft guide said, then it could get rougher, possibly increasing the danger of the hydraulics.

We steered into a wide section of the river, calm and dark. The guide encouraged us to get out and swim. It was hot, and the smooth, inky water was inviting. I hesitated, but mindful of my life vest, I dipped myself out into the river. I knew I would not sink, but still, I realized I could grab the ropes woven around the sides of the raft.

Once in the water, I tread lightly, never letting go of the ropes. I could not see more than two or three inches below the surface. It reminded me of octopus ink I'd seen on television nature shows. I turned toward the guide still sitting in the raft, his oar across his lap. "How deep is the river here?" I asked.

"Oh, about 100 feet. There are places through here with entire small towns underwater. When they dammed the river, everyone had to leave their homes. Houses, churches, schools, government buildings. Wooden structures I imagine are rotted by now."

I looked back down to the water where I treaded. Were ghosts down there, ready to pull the living under, angry over losing their homes, their livelihoods? I couldn't blame them.

"They say there are channel cats down there as big as school busses," the river guide told me now, looking at my hand firmly gripping the raft's ropes. I knew about catfish supposedly undisturbed in their growth, troweling at the bottom of lakes and rivers growing to enormous sizes.

"Catfish as big as a bus?" I scoffed, now trying to wipe the smirk off his face. He jerked his eyes away from me and didn't answer.

He called to us to re-board. We paddled around the bend and suddenly we heard the roar of big rapids. All too soon we were headed straight for a category four rapid. "Paddle right! Paddle right! Keep paddling right!"

He was steering us toward what we'd been warned in our safety talk to avoid: a massive hydraulic. I thought about previous years when rafters were pulled under and drowned. Sometimes, it took weeks before their bodies were retrieved, as divers risked their lives to recover the rafter or kayaker.

The raft guide screamed: "YOU! On the left! Paddle, paddle, paddle!" But I couldn't move. Directly ahead of us was a huge rock, standing in the river like a Stonehenge upright, so wide it blocked the view ahead. And then BOOM! Like an explosion of dynamite, we hit the boulder. It felt like running headlong into a concrete wall. The jolt came through us fast and hard. The raft's front pitched up, almost perpendicular. I reached out to cling to the ropes as if I were on a bucking bronco. Two rafters on the right side, a married couple, were tossed out like toys pitched in the air by a dog. I felt a blast of pain on my left shin. The 10-pound lunch bucket they pack for rafters had come down on my leg, gashing it open.

Our raft pitched to the right, with the bow splashing down on the rough water. I was able to see the two who were tossed out. The woman clung to the ropes of the raft, as she had somehow managed to grab them as she sailed up and then back down. The husband wasn't so lucky. A non-swimmer, he'd been thrown out to the middle of the river. He remembered to roll onto his back, feet pointed down river, and sail on top the rapids. The guide immediately threw him a bag with a rope coiled inside. The hapless, river-tossed rafter grabbed the bag and hung on. The guide and another man reeled him back into the raft. The woman clambered back inside as well. Now, we were drifting, with no one paddling as we came out of the rapids.

Once everyone was settled back in place, I pointed to my injured leg, blood running onto the bottom of the raft. The guide put his oar down and came toward me, barely glancing at my leg. "That's going to leave a hell of a knot. If you'd paddled like I told you that wouldn't have happened." I shot a glance at my husband to see if he'd heard the guide. He shrugged. I was incredulous the guide tried to blame this incident on me. The three of us, two men and me, on the left had all frozen with our paddles in hand as the rock loomed above us. I was not the only one paralyzed in place.

The guide said nothing to anyone else and returned to his station at the back of the raft. We paddled in silence through a category three rapid then a few category two rapids. We finally steered toward the shoreline to stop for lunch. I hobbled out, speaking to no one, least of all my lack-of-support husband. He came over, "Does it still hurt?" I looked at the gash, now swollen the size of a hen's egg.

"What the hell do you think?" I snapped. I took my sandwich over to a lone rock and sat down to eat it. I had no patience for him maintaining his "manly" toughness and silence in the face of what had happened.

The rapids for the remainder of the trip were mild, categories one or two. Some were nothing more than ripples. Finally, after two more hours of paddling in the hot sun, we disembarked for our bus ride back to the river rafting basecamp. Once there, I went to the ladies room to wash the dried blood off my leg. It throbbed.

I came out to see and hear two men from our raft talking. "He admitted there were three ways you can steer down the river—a mild, a bit rougher, and then a really rough passage. He said he chose the really rough because he was bored." The other man nodded and said, "He thinks he's a cowboy, I guess. Gonna tame the wild bull." The other man agreed. "Yee Haw! Cowboy on the river!" They moved away toward the counter to pay for the snacks they'd picked up.

On the drive home, my husband asked me why I was so quiet. I told him what I'd overhead the two men say. I said, "I saw you leaning your weight onto the bow, so the ride would be rougher. The more fun for you, I suppose. Or maybe just more dangerous."

"I don't know about more dangerous . . . just more fun, yeah."

"For you. If you were alone, or with people more experienced, okay. Fine. Have fun. But you knew there were non-swimmers and you knew about hydraulics, right? What if the man who went overboard got pulled into a hydraulic. It happens every year. Maybe the stupid guide's *boredom* is how people drown. Last year was fun. We rode the rapids safely and it was a wild ride. Dude. Not everything needs to be made more dangerous to have fun."

My husband remained silent. *What could he say? I'm sure he thought I was a wimp. Fine. Think it. I'm at least alive, albeit injured.*

For several nights following, then intermittently over the years, I remembered that rafting trip, shuddering again and again over the real possible ending we could have had. I imagined being dragged down under the water, pounded and slammed against a giant boulder. Would I have passed out before I drowned, or would I have suffered my throat burning, a strangling. For how long?

My husband went on the yearly rafting trips several more times. I didn't ask him how it went. He came home; it was answer enough.

Videy (Viðey) Island

The ferry's engine vibrated up through our padded seats as we chugged across a channel on the North Atlantic Ocean between the mainland and the island. The eight or so fellow passengers studied their I-Phones, looked at maps, or gazed out to the sea on our left. I initially traveled to Iceland for a writer's conference, but once I'd discharged my duties by reading my paper at a roundtable, attended a panel session and one keynote address, I couldn't wait to spring myself free to explore. I could neither afford time nor money to travel more deeply into the sparsely populated interior of Iceland, so this seven-minute trip to Viðey Island, or Videy as we English speakers called it, had to suffice. I had long been seeking a way to leave the crowds and here was my opportunity.

I watched out the ferry's windows as the island grew nearer. The engine throttled down and the boat slowed as the pilot eased it against the dock. My thoughts settled on why I had come to Iceland and how I wanted to spend my time: not in university teacher mode, now that I had done my due diligence at a writing conference, but in a writerly reverie. Exploring made me feel like playing hooky from the rest of the conference, but the island represented a chance to slow down. On this spit of land, where nothing is, I could think of something other than what feels like my nonstop obligation to others.

I patted my purse where my brand new, blank journal rested. I imagined I'd ramble the expanse of the mile square as if the island belonged to me, like Robinson Crusoe, and then sit, stare out to sea, and write. No one needed me. No one knew I was here, save they knew I was in Iceland.

My travel guidebook said Videy Island has virtually nothing on it, with the land mass only a mile square. A few dilapidated houses remained, along with the governor's residence from the 1790s, turned into a café; a small white church; and a building housing an H-vac system. From the air, the shape of the island looks like a cat perched on top a fencepost. It's actually considered two islands, with an isthmus in between. Colonized by the Vikings in 900 CE, an Augustine Monastery flourished from the 13th to the 16th centuries. The island supported ship-building enterprises from just after the turn of the 20th century to the 1950s, with a top population of 138 residents. It must have been quite crowded but looking at the island now little evidence remains of a once bustling industry. The ship-building shifted to Reykjavik Harbor, allowing the island to revert to grass, devoid of trees, as is much of Iceland. It became a sanctuary where thirty bird species find food and nesting sites. If visitors are lucky, they'll spy a colony of seals playing on the beaches or spot a whale breaching a short distance away. Reviewers who visited Videy lamented there was "nothing there." A few said it offered little but tufts of grass and goose poop in abundance. One reviewer even titled his entry: "Find something else to do."

♦

The ferry docked and my boatmates and I disembarked. I stopped to admire two large, pale starfish attached to the dock's underwater supports. I wondered if they dined on barnacles because I'd never seen so many lodged on one structure. Barnacles upon barnacles—clearly a clannish crustacean, and as I had read, permanently attached. They would spend their lives cemented to the dock's pylons, never leaving home, or saying goodbye to Mom in order to find a more exciting neighborhood, even perhaps a better paying job.

My thoughts turned to when I began college at 36, where I rediscovered my joy of reading, and the realization I could write reasonably well—*like millions of others* came the frequent chastisement from my own mind. But then life accelerated, and went on and on, new goals to be reached. Where is my center? I wondered as I considered the starfish's legs raying out from its plump belly. I felt like those barnacles, piles upon piles of the same. A giant mass of stuff, moving, but going nowhere.

Walking up the dock, I glanced across the narrow channel, noting the Látrabjarg Cliffs (Jargon Cliffs as I thought of them because I could neither read nor pronounce Icelandic). The cliff's rock face of black pumice looked like a cindered moon surface, a reminder

Iceland is volcanic. The surface appeared to me as a *tabula rasa*—a darkscape, barren.

Approaching the slope's top, I walked into the brilliant little white church. On my rambles around Reykjavik, I had noticed many buildings in Iceland are stark white—I suppose to capture more warmth—and to gather any light from the low-slung sun.

In juxtaposition to the dark pumice, the white church reminded me of a clean, uncluttered mind, an inviting space for clarity. A soft, bluish glow bathed the interior of the small church. I am not religious, yet I appreciated the cloistered feeling, the soft light filtering through the old windowpanes.

Exiting the church, I stopped to consider the view of Reykjavik from the island. Heavily populated with homes and businesses spiraling upwards around a large hill, your eye is led up to the large stone church at the top, its spire towering, almost spindly. I thought of Dante's *Inferno*, from his *Divine Comedy,* only in his case, images of Dante's literary creation depict rings spiraling down into the bowels of Hell. Dante *Alighieri,* a man who broke ranks with the officially approved Latin and wrote in a Tuscan vernacular—was a rebel. Only such a freed soul as Dante could imagine and write about the fate of us sinners. I identified with his rebellion, but I'm hardly slouching toward Bethlehem. I thought: *I am glad I am alone on*

Videy Island and in Iceland, and I tingled at the thought of my own tiny, inward, rebellion to travel alone, in a land where I could neither read nor write the language. I was no spring chicken and the world is far more dangerous.

◆

All the other passengers had scattered, but I suddenly sensed someone standing to my left. I glanced over at a young woman, tall, with long curly, light brown hair. She studied a map of the island. Glancing up, she looked at me and smiled.

"Wanna join me a bit of the way?" she asked as she folded her map and stowed it in her backpack. She seemed like a nice person. She told me her name was Valerie. I said yes.

As I walked beside her away from the few dwellings and any other people, I marveled at my answer: easy, unhesitating. I had come to this island for solitude and here I stumbled alongside this stranger, almost half running because her legs were long and her strides far apart. She chattered quietly, staring forward to the path. I had to keep trotting to lessen the space between us in order to hear her. Valerie grew up in Washington, DC. I learned she'd spent the last six years in England, attending Oxford until she finished her dissertation about islands being inundated by rising sea waters.

"You study global climate change, then?" I asked, puffing a bit from the exertion of keeping up with her.

"Well . . ." her voice trailed off as we came to an edge of the island and looked at the beach, perhaps 50 feet below. "Maybe," she finally said. I pondered her cryptic answer when she turned and headed away from the edge and across a field of tufted grass, off the path. I stayed behind her, again straining to hear what she said, fearing an ankle sprain as I tumbled off the top of tuft after tuft.

When I was a child, I walked into woods on my grandparents' farm and loved inhaling the primal smell of a forest teeming with life, free of concern about my family's alcoholism and its anger, their backbiting jealousies I little understood but instinctively sensed drove the adults around me. The forest where a little girl learns keeping her mouth shut and doing as told meant peace. I loved the silence of the forest, the chaos caused by the adults in my life temporarily forgotten.

Now, I was on no leisurely, contemplative walk, yet I continued behind Valerie when we again stepped on the fine-gravel path, headed toward the west end of the island and the isthmus. Patches of bright yellow marigolds, Mother Mary's gold, spread out before us, like a carpet of saffron.

Straining to hear her again. I caught: "My mom loves to read. So do I. What do you do?"

"Write," I answered, growing more breathless. "And teach. I have a family . . ." huff, puff. Why didn't I ask her to slow down? But no, she wasn't hurrying. Her leg length and my leg length—I felt like half her height and twice her age . . ..

She stopped then pivoted around to face me. "Oh! Do you have a book published?"

I pulled up short. "Yes," I strangled out, breathing hard now. I was inordinately pleased we'd stopped walking. "I do. I finally got my memoir published."

"Oh! Can I read it?"

"Um, yes. It's on Amazon as well as from my university publisher . . ."

"What's the title?"

"It's *Riding on Comets*." She oohed about the title and asked how I'd come to name it.

"My parents were unable to follow their dreams because of poverty. They had to quit school after the 10th grade to go to work. But they wanted to make sure I followed my dreams. Their wish was to lift me up to something extraordinary, like riding a comet. I also chose comets as a symbol because my dad studied the night sky, taught me constellations." I sighed. I could feel my heart slow as I talked. Valerie was watching birds wheel over our heads, and I suddenly felt I was boring to this young woman. I finished lamely, "I always assumed I would soar to great success . . . or arrive in town like some spur-jangling hero riding a white horse to set things right. Then ride off into the sunset—alone." I laughed. I was relieved to hear her laugh, too.

I felt disoriented and a bit silly. The whole speech sounded so . . . manufactured, a published author spiel.

Valerie pulled her backpack off and dug around, coming up with a small notebook and a pen. She wrote the title down and my name. "I'll find it," she said then whirled around, headed west again, talking, mumbling. I jolted with irritation finally chafing at my self-betrayal. *What is wrong with discussing my book? Wasn't this practiced spiel what I had learned to do? Why didn't I just say: my parents were poor. They wanted me to succeed. They raised me to believe the sky had no limit.* I felt the disciplined me and the unstructured me war in my brain.

I slowed my pace to my normal stride. I inhaled more deeply, further quieting my breath and heartbeat. I became aware of my softer footfall on the path. I watched as Valerie strode forward.

Still yet I see her far-reaching step, moving resolute. Maybe I could see remnants of my young self from the long lens of time filtered through her. She seemed so unformed, like her vagueness about her dissertation. How on earth can you be vague about a dissertation after it's completed? But for a moment, I envied her standing at the beginning, still deciding what she would be, what she would come to believe. I hoped she always cared less for others' opinions and more concerned with what she thinks. I sensed she was on a good path.

That's when I noticed the training of my mind. Naturally curious as a child, curiosity came filtered through the regimen of education and teaching, bedfellows leading to questions, which led to more questions, which made me think of new ideas, and to realize heretofore unknown realizations. I was trained, readily accepting the training, to ask the obvious questions then to ask, through association, ever more deeply probing questions. Training is, in and of itself, a good thing.

Yet, when I was little, I simply admired the many legs of a millipede without wondering about the purpose of so many legs, other than to walk differently. Or to climb. To explore. It is wonderful, what I've done with my mind, as have many. But now I had arrived where I have to ask: to what end? How has all this training led me to miss the greater fact of contentment from all the answers? Trained to ask, but not so well trained to render it into anything other than turning around and teaching my students. My curiosity had heaven wrung out of it. Exactly when had I lost my ability to be awestruck, to stand and bathe in the glow of wonderment? This island was helping me remember.

♦

Valerie stopped at the edge of the island, beside a pair of columnar basalt stones, an art installation called *Áfangar*, meaning "stages." Again, I remembered the history of these stones from the travel guide. The pairs were installed by the American Minimalist artist Richard Serra. Nine pairs of columns, each framing a different view: the cliffs, Reykjavik, the North Atlantic. In my guidebook I had read about the artist; the work is a creation of preciseness, and environmental commentary, placed according to strict mathematical criteria. Each time visitors come to a "portal" they are to stop, take in where they are, think about where they've been, maybe where they're going. Or perhaps, just to stare. What an unexpected contrast: mathematical rigidity giving way to dreaming.

With slow, measured steps, I caught up to Valerie. I reached out to one of the basalt pairs. I rubbed my hand along the stone's surface, thinking they looked like blown-off-course uprights from Stonehenge. Then Valerie faded from my thoughts, along with the surroundings. Behind us, unseen birds began to call sounding like the meadow-nesting killdeer in my home state.

♦

Valerie's voice broke through my reverie. I turned toward her.

"Yoko Ono's Peace Tower is next on my list," she was saying as she turned her map upside down, then sideways. "Wanna go see it?"

I decided I'd stay with Valerie just a bit longer, shored up with my new-found, still unformed determinations, but recognizing the confusion had ebbed, the advantage of having lived a while—you learn to move through surprising changes, knowing you aren't going to die once fantastic realization arrives. I suddenly felt a thrill shoot through me thinking of the sparseness of this island, against which I was composing and coalescing new thoughts, perhaps even echoing them against the retreating back of sweet Valerie, thoughts slipping into my consciousness on little cat feet.

"Sure," I said of the offer to go see the tower. "I've googled and read about it. Yoko Ono erected it in honor of John Lennon's birthday." We turned to skirt along the outer edge of the Island then inward to a brief rise on the path. We saw an object ahead resembling a large, squat storage tank. As we neared the structure, we could make out the words *Imagine Peace* etched into a smooth white tile. Randomly, other tiles held words, most of which I couldn't read and as it turns out "imagine peace" is carved in 24 languages. The idea of the tower began with John Lennon back in 1967 when he wanted one erected in his garden. Eventually, Yoko had it built on Videy Island in 2006. The tower is lit on John's birthday, October 9, and glows until December 8, the anniversary of John's death. It consists of several large, round lights inside the base of the tank, pointed up, angled just enough for the individual beams to travel separately for a while then unite and shine together into the heavens.

You may say I'm a dreamer.

Valerie toured around the small tower once then said, "I'm going to walk back now toward the café. I think I'll skip going across the isthmus, maybe then go toward the east end of the island. Want to come with me?"

For once, I said nothing. But I turned to follow her. As we walked away I looked back at the squat tower, trying to decide if it represented the rebel Beatle. My eyes lifted to the wild, cold ocean.

♦

Finally, we arrived at the café, the former Governor's mansion. Valerie and I visited the restroom downstairs, a large, cavernous room echoing our steps on the terrazzo floor. When we came back upstairs, I spied the small kitchen and smelled the aroma of strong coffee. Valerie stood facing me; now I looked fully at her face, her soft blue eyes, as she shifted her backpack, catching a strap on a curl of hair. Her smile so sweet. One "obligation" I will never abandon: acknowledge someone's nature and honor it by listening, and perhaps, it is okay to accompany them a short way on their journey. I sighed into the thought. Suddenly I felt my shoulders lower, the tension ease.

I took a deep breath and smiled. "Valerie, I'm going to stay here, in the café, and buy a coffee. I want to write in my journal—just sit quietly. I'll see you on the ferry back."

She shrugged then smiled, saying okay. She turned on her heel and headed out the door into the sunshine. I never saw Valerie again.

💧

I was the only customer in the cafe. I sat in the Icelandic sun shining through the window, the brightest it'd been since I'd arrived in Iceland five days previously. In a small, brown ceramic cup, a barista had placed cut marigolds and set it, like an offering, in the middle of my table. I pulled out my journal and my favorite pen. A letter to my parents, gone over 20 years.

"Dear Mom and Dad,

I rode my comet for a few years. no decades. I forgot to look at anything but the comet. But lately, I've come to remember the view up here is pretty spectacular. It is awe inspiring, it is wondrous."

Tossing Jim from the Bridge

After my plane landed in Ireland, I was to meet my driver, Batty, and a woman named Katy for the trip to Anam Cara, a writer's retreat on the Beara Peninsula. I didn't know what Batty or Katy looked like, but Shannon Airport is small, so I felt confident I'd figure it out.

Once I retrieved my luggage, I ventured toward the airport lobby to see a line of men holding paper signs, each with names in large type, but none with mine. Then I saw a man to the back of the group who swayed from foot to foot. He had a soft, folded face and juggled a cell phone and a piece of lined notebook paper. I stepped closer and leaned in to read: in shaky handwriting in light blue ink was PLESKA. Ahh, he had to be Batty. He noticed me peering closely at the paper and he said into his cell phone, "Ah, she's here. I've got her now. Thanks, Sue." I recognized Sue as the name of the owner of the writer's retreat where Katy and I were headed.

He greeted me and told me Katy had arrived and was waiting outside. He grabbed my suitcase and out we went. I glanced around for Katy, who I imagined as a young, petite blonde. She was petite, but her hair was white and she looked to be in her mid-70s, with a lovely, warm smile. We greeted one another. Batty loaded our luggage in the trunk, and then tucked Katy and me in the back seat and off we went, flying at incredibly fast speeds along narrow roads on the wrong side—well, the wrong side to me, anyway. It was disconcerting to have Batty turn around often to chat, but I was so tired I decided to leave our safety to the fates and to the unknown driving skills of a man called Batty.

Ireland's villages hug the highway, with the houses' front doors barely two feet away from the road. I imagined what might happen should I live in such a place and stumble about in the morning. I could become a good-sized hood ornament. Soon enough my sight fell on green fields which glowed more neon than in my native West Virginia. Yet, I hardly noticed much more as we sped toward the south of Ireland. I had not slept on the long over-night flight, flying from Charleston, West Virginia, via Philadelphia. I was crammed against the window in a row of three seats, with a big burly guy in the middle whose wide shoulders signaled a linebacker 50 years earlier and his tiny wife perched like a little blue bird on the aisle seat. The plane was hot and I spent the entire night with my right arm over my chest as there was nowhere else to place it. Katy, in contrast, flying in from Chicago, was bright and chipper and chattered steadily, having slept, she said, like a baby on the long flight. I tried not to resent her, as she was a good bit older than I and I was always taught to respect my elders.

We stopped in route for refreshments at a small white cottage with a huge window toward the back of the house, which showcased a stunning, flower-filled garden and grazing sheep in the pasture beyond. We drank Barry's tea and ate freshly-baked scones. Batty engaged the proprietor in a lengthy conversation about cousins and aunts and uncles and mothers and fathers, and I gathered they'd known each other for quite a long time. I asked Batty about it when we got back in the car. "Oh no," he said. "We just met." That's how it is in Ireland, sort of like West Virginia: who do you know in common? We think in terms of relations. We ask: "Are you Mildred's boy?" or "Do I know your Uncle Bing?" "Are you from the Hodges up Rider's Creek or the ones with money over in Winfield?" Who you are related to might tell us a world about you.

We journeyed on and I was feeling quite woozy. Despite the fact I wanted to ogle the beautiful scenery, the colorful houses, the sheep and cattle in rock-strewn countryside, my head dropped back on the seat rest, and I drifted in and out of a deep sleep for the remainder of the trip. My head did pop up once when I heard Katy brightly say something about bringing ashes with her.

Ashes?

Katy's husband aged 87 (turns out she was 81) had passed away five months earlier. She was bringing his ashes to Ireland because he'd been in country many times to golf, and he wanted a portion of his remains scattered there. Katy is a writer, so she combined the writing retreat at Anam Cara with the opportunity to complete her husband Jim's wishes.

"You can travel overseas with ashes?" I queried.

"Oh sure!" Katy said. "Fill out a few papers and it's done!" *I'll be damned!* I thought. *Who knew?*

Too exhausted to absorb much more than that interesting fact, back to sleep I went.

Once at Anam Cara, a long, ranch-style house sitting just above the banks of the River Kenmare (you can hear its rumble even inside the house), Katy and I met our fellow classmates: a third American, Lisa, and two Irish women, Breda and Christine. We were there for a week of writing with Irish author Marion Reynolds. The land surrounding Anam Cara is astoundingly beautiful. Coulagh Bay shimmered in the near distance and the ocean beyond faded into mists. I knew this would be an inspiring place and time.

The six of us quickly fell into a camaraderie born of a common goal of writing and being over 50. Katy told our class of her mission with the ashes the first evening, and said she was thinking of spreading her beloved Jim in the river. She was going down over the hill from the house the next afternoon to scout out a place. None of us would hear of her going alone. We would help Katy celebrate her husband and their long marriage and see Jim off in proper style. As Christine, the tall, sail-boating, former nurse said, "You have no family here, Katy. We can't let you do that alone. We'll be your family."

Later in the week, on a rainy afternoon, we approached the long stairs down to the river, raging high and out of its banks due to a downpour the previous day. As we descended the steps, we sang over and over: "I will be with you always; always I will be with you." On approaching the river, waterfalls thundered so loud we nearly had to shout to one another to be heard. As we approached the river's edge, I noticed foam swirling in eddies in a small pool between rocks near the bank. The cataracts spilled down from three different heights in a rush to the ocean. Deep green water plummeted over light grey, massive limestone boulders. When I had observed the river's head waters a couple days earlier, in the nearby town of Eyeries, it had been no more than a stream. Now, the stream had swollen to five times its size

Our final destination was a small bridge leading from the riverbank to a small island in the middle of the river. The water flowed on to the Bay and then to the North Atlantic, but first, we stopped at river's edge, a ways away from the falls, where it was quieter. Each of us was to read a poem of our choice in honor of Jim. All the ladies chose poems they had written during the week in our workshops. As

I'm a prose writer, I chose to read Mary Oliver's poem *Heron Rises from a Dark Summer Pond.* It was a somber, sweet tribute as we stood in a tight knot, Irish rain softly pelting our hoods and jackets.

Then we proceeded to the bridge. We climbed its stairs and were suspended over a quiet, shallow section which flowed steadily on to the bay. The water had turned from dark green to brown. Katy reminisced about Jim, what he'd been like and had enjoyed. She and Jim had a long life together, building family and navigating life's peccadilloes as we all do. Then she brought out of her backpack a purple golf towel she'd brought from home and sewed into a carrier for Jim's ashes, which the crematorium had bagged in two, gallon-sized, zip lock baggies.

Taking a deep breath, Katy, teary-eyed, tipped the golf towel bag over the bridge's rail and dumped Jim out. Down he fell to the river below, intact inside the plastic, landing like a stone in the middle of the river. A stone clearly not going to budge.

All six of us were stunned to quiet for a few seconds then all six of us said at once: "oh no!"

Breda said, "Ach! No plastic allowed in the sea!" (The Irish are very environmentally conscious.)

My thinking diverted to our beleaguered American environment, and I was mentally picturing the landfills full of sandwich bags and plastic straws, when I began to hear stifled snickers, and other quiet sounds of willing oneself to not laugh.

A giggle rose in me, but before we could laugh out loud, we suddenly noticed Christine scrambling down the bridge stairs on the other end and striding to the riverbank. With her tall black "wellies" (Wellington boots) to protect her, she stepped out into the river, bent and retrieved the plastic bags and was back on the bridge before any of us had a chance to realize fully what was happening. I looked at Katy. Her initial stunned look shifted to a wide grin.

Katy took the bags and this time unzipped them and down drifted Jim into the River Kenmare. Some of his ashes caught on the soft Irish air, but the bulk landed in the water. We watched as his ashes spread slowly onward, toward the bay and flowed out to the ocean. I studied the place where Jim's ashes had landed noting their cream color against the dark brown river water looked for all the world like the foam on a glass of Guinness. I didn't know for sure, but I bet Jim would have liked the imagery. He certainly had loved Ireland, especially their beautiful golf courses.

And then we were all crying. We hugged each other then chattered all at once, continuing our noise all the way back up the hillside stairs, back to Anam Cara, which means "dear soul" in Irish. We stopped on the patio and opened a couple bottles of wine. We saluted Jim and Katy, and she said, "When I tell my family about this moment, though, I'll not tell them at first about the unsuccessful tossing of Jim into the river in his zip lock baggy. I'll keep it solemn until later. Then I'll tell them."

I thought: ahh, not in West Virginia, a region heavily influenced by immigrating Irish in the 19th century. The Irish still have wakes for their deceased, an occasion celebrated with libation, the best personal stories, and laughter ringing throughout the house where the dearly departed rests until the proper, solemn funeral. Perhaps an attitude we Appalachians have retained is to enjoy the funnier aspects of the deceased's life at the time of death. Well, some of us.

That evening, I listened to my classmates' talk as we polished off several bottles of wine. This was something else about my trip, other than the immediate bonding of us all: the delicious fresh meals three times a day and the copious amount of wine in the evenings. We celebrated the writing we'd accomplished during the day and enthused about the incredibly beautiful and inspiring landscape and listened to Irish stories and American stories. But for the remaining nights, the famous tossing from the bridge story reigned paramount. None of us had previously taken part of scattering ashes, but this incident would stay in our memories a long time. The more wine we drank the louder we laughed over poor Jim landing like a plastic fortified rock.

Eventually, relaxed from the wine, or perhaps a bit fuzzy from the wine, my head dropped back on the couch cushion, and I thought about my own mother's death and funeral. I had not opted for cremation and ashes, as she and Dad had purchased mausoleum crypts, and I didn't think about the dust to dust aspect, but rather morbidly, decayed flesh to bones. I regretted I hadn't thought of a wake but should have as my mother was the queen of wit and comedic timing; just recounting her funny stories would fill the evening with joy. Since she wasn't cremated, I missed the chance to have scattered my mother's ashes over a few yard sales, because shopping was truly what she loved. I even dreamed of her in Heaven once, happily laden with clever yard sale finds. We can't stay solemn long when it comes to death, as we never did in life. I thought: *We endure because we can laugh.*

When my mom died, after much illness and pain, my aunt and I planned her funeral. We and other close family members arrived an hour before the service to be alone with Mom in her casket. My aunt and I approached the open coffin and I felt more dread than I had ever experienced. By the coffin's side I looked, not down at my mother, but up the wall on the other side, toward the ceiling, dreading to look down upon her. But just then I heard my aunt's sharp intake of breath. She grabbed my arm and said, "Your mother is going to kill you! Oh Lord, probably me too!" Startled and confused, I suddenly looked down at Mom. Other than she looked so pitifully thin, due to the cancer, she looked okay, if one can say it. "What do you mean?" I asked my aunt.

She practically hissed, "You brought the wrong wig!"

"What? You told me to bring the one in the box!"

"She must have switched them out. She kept her most expensive, best-looking wig in the one wig box she had. She insisted we use that one!"

We were silent for a moment, both considering the consequences when we are called from the roll up yonder. My aunt was right. She would kill us both. Mom was always fastidious about her hair. It was never styled to suit her and she fussed every day, insisting my aunt perm her hair each month, sometimes to a frizzed, even melted effect. Daily she wielded her mighty curling iron, invariably burning her neck or cheek with it. I used to stuff her Christmas stocking with burn cream. I often said it was a wonder she had any hair left. I never saw it mussed but once when she was sick and in the hospital. Then it all fell out with chemo treatments, but still she immediately bought several wigs and stylish turbans. She was determined to be properly coiffed, in death as in life. Even if it was the heavenly realm, my goose would be thoroughly cooked when she saw me.

At that moment, standing with my head hung in shame, before my deceased mother, my aunt and I did the unthinkable. We laughed, the absurd reckoning we imagined rubbing against our funny bones. Quickly covering our mouths to stifle the giggles, we peeked around us to see if anyone had noticed. I know seeing me from behind someone might have thought my shoulders were shaking with crying. Once the tears of laughter eased, then came the crying tears of sorrow. But it felt different. The depths of despair were not so deep; the laughter had softened the blow.

When my golf-loving uncle died, his children loaded his casket with golf balls, golf tees, and his favorite putter. The minister joked my uncle should be buried on the 17th green, his favorite. When my dad died, several of us family members stifled laughs when the minister, who did not know my father, talked about my dad's clean-living. My dad was a raging alcoholic. We muttered: Is he at the right funeral?

When a family member or friend dies, we gather at someone's house and unless a demise was unexpected or to a young person or due to a tragedy, we eat food till our bellies bulge and tell stories till our sides ache from laughing. We mean no disrespect. Besides, it's in our genes and our history. I'd read about Appalachian humor, of which West Virginia is wholly within this storied region, was influenced by Calvinistic belief (usually considered austere) which says everyone is flawed and it's up to each of us to note our flaws and find a way, through humor, to help the dear soul recognize his own foibles. How else could one become humble?

I came out of my reverie to note my classmates sharing stories of their respective experience with funerals. I let my thoughts drift again about memorial humor until they sloshed around in my mind. Our society has become too sad, everything is too sacred. We laugh, true, but then we are burdened with what others must think, seemingly thanks to social media, the platform where judgment is immediate. It's not about disrespect; it is about loving life and all our foibles. It's about humility, which has gone the way of common sense—into that great good night.

It takes a good ash-tossing to realize the importance of life, and Jim's near miss gave me the chance to think about my own demise. There were my myriad accomplishments the people at my memorial could note. My roles as wife and mother, daughter and cousin, friend. My charitable works, my writing, my devotion to my beloved pets. Ahh, how solemn it would all be . . . I let the scenario play out and the images swam among the flotsam and jetsam of life's achievements. Then I came awake with this realization: please, powers that be: Let'em laugh. Let'em guffaw. Let'em remember me with mirth until their sides ache. Then I'll know they loved me.

I will be with you always, always I will be with you.

Water Sign

Seated in front of me at a card table, a plump woman clicked on the cassette tape player.

"Scorpios are water signs," the psychic said, wiggling on the folding chair. She was patting the Tarot cards she'd laid out in front of me on the card table.

"They often submerge in their surroundings, seeking the hidden emotional reality, a built-in sonar for reading a mood. At their best, they are a healing force that brings people together—at their worst, they are psychic vampires, able to manipulate and drain the life force of those closest to them."

I squirmed in *my* seat. "Oh dear. That sounds awful . . ."

The card reader shrugged, smiled at me, "Well, at your worst, that is. That doesn't mean you fall to such a level, but just so you know, and watch for it. You're aware of your power, though. Scorps can sense "vibes" from others. Sense what they really mean rather than what the others do or say. They have to work harder to maintain their boundaries, surprisingly, given they are a force of nature. It's strange Scorpio is a fixed sign, which means you go deep with a fixed focus. You'd think being a water sign you'd be fluid, wouldn't you?" She laughed. I grinned, not sure what all the conjecture meant.

"That sounds like a dog with a bone . . ." I managed to say.

"Yes, to some extent. You don't let go until you're satisfied you know all there is to know. But like that dog with a bone, you do sometimes don't know when to let go. It can keep you from seeing what's really there . . .

"Water signs soften the edges of the mundane by adding to it emotional meaning. Nothing is what it seems to you Scorps. Your feelings can lead you into the arts, like writers, musicians, and actors. Many of these artists are Scorps.

Well, one thing makes sense. I am a writer.

"Water is a formless element on its own, and that's why those with this sign are so quickly shaped by their relationships to others. They need time alone to remember where they end and others begin. These are people who need people, but also need solitude, to be restored."

"I do need people but on my own terms," I blurted. "I mean, I don't mean that as harsh as it sounds. I mean the world is too much with us, at times. I'm slow to trust and once trust is broken . . . I don't find it easy to trust again." I was rambling.

"Who does, sweetie?" The psychic snorted and patted the cards again, lifting one then another to consider them.

"Scorps don't have a tolerance for danger they did not bring on themselves." She nodded her head as if to reinforce the statement. And it called to mind white water rafting.

"Scorps are the most stubborn of the water signs. They will move heaven and hell to get their own way. That can be damaging to a relationship. You need to think about that . . ." She looked from the cards to me, held me in her gaze a moment. I felt exposed.

"But you . . . " now she clicked her tongue and fondled the cards again. "You float out and beyond the troubled waters, beyond the shores. You come back better, stronger. You see, Scorps are fearless, if they are the ones in control. Now, it doesn't mean, especially as a water sign, you don't have fears. Sometimes you are awash in them. But after the initial shock, you suddenly power up, something within you gathers steam. You inhale and go after whatever is frightening you, and when you decide to, lookout! I would not want to be tethered to you if you decide to make someone see the error of their ways." I could swear she shuddered.

"What sign is your husband?" Although I never said I had one, she must have guessed.

"He's an Aquarius."

"Perfect! He'll roll with the punches. He'll also be your greatest challenge, but he, too, will keep you from floating off this earth. He is not sentimental toward you."

No shit.

"Honey, I just read the cards. They say what they're going to say, and I have no control. I don't manipulate them." *Was she sensing my uneasiness? No, probably reading my facial expressions.*

She sighed and leaned back, with one final pat on the cards. "You see, you already know all this, don't you?" She didn't give me time to answer.

"You didn't ask for advice, but here it is: go sit by the river. Or creek, hell, sit in a bathtub, but it's by water you'll realize the truth of who you are."

She stopped the recorder, removed the cassette and handed it to me.

Submersion

Well, the old card reader maybe had a point. She wasn't old, actually. I don't know, maybe my age. But here I am, getting in a tub of water. I can't expect anything, can I? Then why am I doing this? I prefer showers.

"Shut up! Just get in the damn tub!" My voice echoed around in my newly built bathroom, right off my bedroom. It was to be my sanctuary, even though as it was being built I fought the idea of installing a tub.

"You might regret not having one to soak in," my husband had advised. I caved. I chose a tub, an old cast iron beauty from the antique dealer's bathtub bone yard. Six feet long, with a sloping back, built in 1940, it was in good condition. I peeled a hundred bucks out of my purse, and we loaded the tub in our pickup truck and lugged the 200-pound behemoth home. I chose turquoise paint for the outside and silver for the clawed feet. I bought replica fixtures like what would have been on the tub when new.

I sprinkled in bubble bath. The foam rose to the edge of the tub top when I turned off the faucet. I eased in first one foot, steadied my balance then lifted the other foot over and in. Then I slid down, no mean feat, I discovered. I'm getting old!

I settled against the bath pillow my son-in-law had gifted me for Christmas and admitted the heat felt good on my body. I was grateful because the back of the hard tub was no place to rest your head.

Okay, I am submerged.

Now what? I decided to turn loose my mind, let it roam. No easy task for me—without wine, anyway.

Is this what it feels like to be back in the womb? Warm, sloshy, protected? I thought of my mother, who had me at 11:45 Halloween night. A Halloween baby, I'd heard all my life. I loved it.

Mom said she'd craved ice chips when she was pregnant with me. The power of suggestion is strong, I suppose, as I did as well when I was pregnant with my daughter. Or we both lacked some mineral during pregnancy. It was never addressed with either of us, so who knows?

Unbidden, thoughts of her now crowded in. I splashed a handful of water on my face, but the imagery came fast, albeit in shorthand, breathless. My mother.

Lost her mother when she was 10. Given over to an older brother and his wife, who was an abuser, both physically and emotionally. No one to stand ground for her, and she was so young. Her father, a letch, apparently; she and her sisters locked their doors against him. If he were angry, a two-by-four might come in handy to swing at them. Then marriage at 18 to a man, my father, who was movie star handsome. He worked, supported us, all while mostly raging drunk. She was depressed and hospitalized, electro-shocked, some memory wiped out. Always worried, always fearful of possible danger, even in the most innocent moments. Guarded, but at times, especially when he was at work, she was fun, funny. Hilarious at times. Quick witted. Kind. I knew she loved me. I felt secure amidst instability.

What was I supposed to do with all the memory embedded in me, of her, her life. It was almost as if she instilled in me her experience too. I carried two lives. Sometimes it felt as if I would be pushed under, drowned.

Her sorrow. More than my own.

Once, a small, pixyish woman approached me. She stepped right up to me as if she would embrace me. We'd just left a demonstration of reiki, the act of moving energy around someone else's body to heal. Some nurses are trained in this natural ability we're all supposed to have. The Pixie said, "I'm sorry to bother you, but when I saw you up on the stage, (I was a volunteer for the practicing nurse) I sensed immense sadness in you." She reached out her hand as if to touch my arm but stopped. I was speechless for a moment. I studied her ears sticking out from under short, cropped hair. They were pointed. She perhaps came to my shoulder, and I am short.

She was crying.

"Well, I suppose so," I admitted. "But . . ." I began to rally. "I suppose I've always known, but I choose to use it. I mean (what did I mean?)... I use it to grow in knowledge and strength. I use it to write." I lamely explained.

She sniffled, looking away. She nodded her head. "Okay. I just wanted you to know. I see it."

My bath water had grown cold. I sat for a couple more minutes, still not sure what to do, even years later, with the Pixie's remarks. I have no idea where she came from or where she got off to. I did not see her again. I wondered if she were real. I know she was.

I stood up in the bathtub, again, no mean feat, and reached for a towel.

♦

All noble minded men are inclined to sadness. . . . it is their inward sympathy and consciousness of participation in the sufferings of the human race, to which they belong. ~Aristotle

Water Dreams

Still, I rarely soak in a tub. Work, family, stressful pandemic from a virus where lungs fill, needing a ventilator . . . I don't have time to lie in cooling water and sniff incense, worry I'll forget to blow out candles.

My massage therapist insisted I should soak more often. She said my muscles need to relax. Sitting at a computer all day, grading papers, trying to keep up with Facebook—but who has time?

"Soaking in a tub is how you repair those muscles. And it's close by," she said. "You have to go no farther than your bathroom, since you tell me you have to drive to a park to take a walk. Maybe this will work."

"I don't have time," I complained for the millionth time.

One day, after four hours straight of grading, coping with virtual class meetings, which the students hated, grumbling about tight, achy muscles, I said, "Screw it." I filled my tub with hot water, undressed, and slipped in, sinking down under the water to my neck. Criminy. It felt good. My muscles seemed to relax. I grew sleepy. *God, I hope I don't drown* was my last thought.

♦

My parents sat at an enamel-topped table drinking coffee. Mom had on a black skirt with a pink poodle applique, and Dad's hair was freshly Brylcreemed. Mom rose from the table to come to kiss my cheek. Then sat back down. They smiled at me, as if they were glad to see me, too.

"Am I dead, Mom?"

"Yes. Don't worry. You'll return to life in a moment." *They'd both been gone for so, so long.*

"Sit. Have coffee with us." *I looked at them and noticed a plate of my dad's favorite cookies in the middle of the table, Oreos. Mom pointed to the coffee pot on the stove.*

I couldn't move. I could only drink in the sight. She rose from the table again, and reaching into her skirt pocket, she pulled out a slip of paper, handing it to me. Only one line of text, but the letters were crammed together, unreadable.

OPJWEARGPSERGPWE4LMNOFAO0IJHEAPBNOEP0AONEPOGH

"Will I ever know what your message says?" *I stared at my mother, unable to take my gaze from her beautiful face.*

She nodded, "In time."

◆

I jerked awake from the dream, still submerged in now tepid water. I sat up and concentrated hard on the message still floating in my memory. It was no use. I had no idea what the message said.

The next day, I posted a question on Facebook. I asked about inspiration, what influences us, helps us find ideas to write.

A former writing student, Madison Haley, wrote on my timeline: "When I was your publishing intern, you gave me the best advice I still use to this day for writing: go to the water. I wrote some of my favorite pieces in the early morning, on the beach, sitting on the cold sand, water lapping at my feet. If I can't get to the ocean, I'll listen to water-centered music or stay in the shower."

If you're wondering, I still don't have much time to soak in the tub. But recently, I stood beside a creek, the one from my childhood where I caught minnows in a chipped cup my grandmother gave me. The one where I'm sure the same beloved grandmother, when I was three, threw a burlap bag of kittens in, acquainting me early with the burden of sorrow. The same creek where I waded on hot days feeling the heat of me cool, after my family argued all day. The creek that sheltered small frogs in spring, who'd chorus loudly after a summer storm.

I don't think it is what the crammed-letter message from my mother says, go to the water, but then again, maybe so.

Washed Clean

My aunt Norma's memory is fading. She repeats the same information several times in a conversation, her mind murky on details. On the phone, I asked her what my uncle's middle name was, her brother. She couldn't recall, but I allowed for the fact she is one of 10 children. She is the last one.

I don't know if she remembers almost drowning me in the tub when I was a baby. I'm surprised I don't have a phobia about bathtubs, especially clawfoot ones. Somehow, I accept bathtubs hold danger and serenity, and if you are careful, it is safe.

I have come to terms with the incident. She was almost a child herself, and certainly she feared the anger and anguish of her sister, my mother. It is likely the more time went on it became easier to not tell my mother what happened, especially after witnessing more of Mom's troubled life. I am sure she never wanted to add to it. And as likely, she felt guilt, something she shouldn't have felt.

She was closest to my mother in age. Mom told me when she and Norma were kids, "climbing like monkeys in a tree," they spoke a language they had invented which only they understood, just as twins have been known to do. They were two years apart, so they never shared the watery environs of a womb, but they were always at one another's side in life.

I am grateful she was there when my mother passed away, drowning in fluids gathering in her lungs. I was on my way, but I could not traverse the eight-hour drive fast enough, in time to be by her bedside. Perhaps it is fitting that the one person she was closest to all her life was the one who watched over her until the end. Perhaps it is a way the universe made things up to her, to me, for the past.

Angels Float on High

Another psychic once told me I had two angels looking out for me from beyond. Both angels, she said, were my grandmothers, my mother's mother and my father's mother. My mother's mother, Lula Florence, died nine years before I was born. "I see her dancing her girls when they were little on the tops of her feet, waltzing around the kitchen to songs on the radio," the psychic said. Later, I asked my aunt about this, as my mother was already gone. Norma said, "Yes, she died when I was 8, but I remember her dancing with each of us younger girls, around in the kitchen, and in the yard she would grab our hands and swing us in the air."

Lula Florence had 10 living children, two more gone via miscarriages. It was hard living, growing food, wringing chicken necks, milking a cow, pulling water up in a bucket from a well. I would never know her, but I learned about her from my mother's stories. A proud woman, a beaten woman, married to a mean man. The wonder is why she stayed, but where was she to go? Her mother had died of the flu in 1920, the left-over legacy of the 1918 flu. My grandmother was a young teen then.

My other grandmother, the one who saved my life with an onion poultice, I loved. I was 39 when she passed. I think about how she saved me, how I am here because of her. With her quick wit and dark sense of humor, she fed me a slice of apple from the blade of a knife. From her I learned to iron clothes, beginning with my grandfather's handkerchiefs, and to can vegetables I helped her pick from her garden. My grandfather drank and for years she drove him around so he wouldn't wreck and kill others.

I know she drowned newborn kittens. Probably dozens over the years. I know it was the times when many people did the same. But at the end of her life, long after my grandfather's death, she saved the last kitten from her cat, Patches, the cat of multiple litters a year. Fluffy was a beauty, a long-haired calico, with a tail as puffy as an ostrich feather. She was my grandmother's companion, the only cat spayed, so the list of drowned kittens stopped.

It is a hazy, brief memory, standing on a wooden bridge over the creek by my grandmother's house. I saw her swing back the burlap bag and fling it out over the creek, where it landed, the water flowing over it as it sank to the bottom. I recall most the feeling in my heart. It was a heaviness in the center of my chest. I closed my eyes and stood for a while, helpless. I don't remember anything else. I know, now, the heaviness lodged inside my body was sadness. It is this sadness, multiplied through the years by many things, the loss of my grandparents, my parents. This is what the Pixie woman sensed in me.

Logically, I know no one cared about kittens long ago. I know had that not been done, there would have been hundreds roaming around the yard, into the hills beyond my grandmother's house. Year after year, more kittens. I know the logic of this then and it has only changed some these days, but it is a little better. Every cat I have saved does not ease my spirit's sorrow, but I am grateful for every animal I can give the chance to have a good life.

One of my last memories of my grandmother is her sitting in her favorite chair in the backyard, cigarette in one hand, a cup of coffee in the other. She transferred the coffee cup to the hand with the cigarette to reach down to pet Fluffy. The sun was shining on the two of them.

I loved her. I think of her swift action to save me, a moment she told me about many times. And I remember her warm smile. Her deep brown eyes. Her chuckle. And my eyes swim in tears.

Grandfather's Mug

My grandfather drank himself to death.

In the mornings, the day began quiet enough. A brown ceramic coffee mug awaited him with the hot brew to begin the day. Cigarette smoke twirled above his head, filtering through his silver hair, like Santa Claus and his pipe. This benevolent figure morphed into something different by evening when the mug was replaced by a bottle of whiskey and a glass of beer to chase it. By nightfall, his words were slurred, his hand unsteady in reaching for the bottle. His tone of voice slid from quiet and thoughtful to challenging and impatient. I thought of my grandfather as that mug—warm and inviting, but he became the bottle, labeled with unhealthy contents, beads of sweat dribbling down the sides. I asked my father once what his dad expected out of life, what did he dream might happen. "Dad didn't think about anything that I know of" he said. "All he was concerned about was his next bottle of whiskey." How does one go through a life with no dreams?

Swallow.

Swallow.

Swallow.

His cup would never runneth over because he was forever emptying it.

Confluence

A feeling of sadness and longing, that is not akin to pain, resembles sorrow only as the mist resembles the rain. ~Henry Wadsworth Longfellow.

After a summer rain, the concrete can sizzle, throw up columns of steam. Droplets roll to the tip of trees' leaves, and if the sun comes out, they shimmer like diamonds. It smells of earth, the rich aroma they call petrichor. In a field close by, the sharp odor of green surrounds you, and mists, cloud tendrils, drift upward from the valleys to the tops of the hills and disappear into the still dark clouds.

The rumble of thunder moves away, and heat lightning flashes up and over the hills, moving east.

Once, in a dream, I was on a child's swing. Suddenly, there was a downpour of rain, forming a sheet of water between me and the rest of the world. Holes appeared making the wall of water seem as if it had the properties of lace. Only in dreams can the physics of life be denied. I continued to swing, kicking my legs back and forth as I watched the rain curtain, the lacy holes remaining steadfast, and through those holes I glimpsed a large building, an abandoned old hotel. I leaned back, hanging on to the swing's chains, as I pumped my legs to go higher and higher. The shabbiness of the building morphed to a refurbished one. I pumped myself higher, now in danger of swinging over the top of the swing set. I looked again and the building was gone, replaced by fields and mountains and a sunrise. Now, the rain stopped and the lace water curtain vanished. I remained in my swing, now still, and beheld the vista. I felt the melancholy come upon me. And then I felt a jolt of excitement.

What is the confluence of flexibility and rigidity, melancholy and joy?

All I know is I live in this state of being. Some days it swings too far into melancholy and other days, the feeling of life breaks upon the shores of joy.

Within this confluence, a person's life flows. We may think of it in bits and pieces, stops and starts, but in reality, when we look back, if we see the confluence of everything which happens to us as springing from the same river of consciousness, of reality, we begin to see patterns and motifs.

I was not wrong when I told the Pixie I used my sadness; it fuels my writing, my way of thinking, the latter in ways I do not realize fully, even now. It's only through recapturing those moments and stitching them together do I see the rivers I have sailed down, or those which have carried me away. I begin to see it all flow together, even if I am not sure how each drop constitutes the stream. I know it will all join in time.

♦

Realization

Last October, I turned 70. When I lift my gaze, I see the distant shore now as I draw closer to it. But I am not ready to haul my boat upon warm sand. I do know this: I am the one who calls out Paddle Left! Paddle Right! to direct my life, and there will be yet more students to whom I advise: Go to the water.

Cat Pleska, a native West Virginian, is an award-winning author, educator, and storyteller. Her memoir, *Riding on Comets* was published by West Virginia University Press. Cat edited four anthologies and her stories and essays have appeared in *The Appalachian Heritage Anthologies, Still: The Journal, Heartwood Magazine, Change 7 Magazine, Women Speak* anthologies, and many others. She teaches in Marshall University's English Department and in the Graduate Humanities Program. She is happy to say she no longer fears bathtubs. Above, she sits in the described turquoise painted claw foot tub, holding her first memoir—it's good reading in the tub! She is the momma to one human, Katie, and six cats.

Thank you!

For reading and commenting on the manuscript: Cater Taylor Seaton, M. Lynne Squires, Debbie Hagan, D. Kate Dooley.

For being the best mom in the world: Jean Hodges

For being the best aunts in the world: Norma Gibson and Gay McCallister

For being the best uncle: Sonny McCallister

For being a thoughtful publisher and friend: Henry Stanton

Previous publications

"One Day on the Lake" *Anthology of Appalachian Writers*, Ann Pancake, ed, vol. 15, 2024

"Strangling Angel" *Anthology of Appalachian Writers*, Dorothy Allison, ed., vol. 13, Shepherd University, 2021.

"Sweet Summer Rain" as "Shelter" in *Riding on Comets: a Memoir*, Abby Freeland, ed., WVUP, 2015

"Tossing Jim from the Bridge" *Still: the Journal, 2018*

"Wash Me Clean" *Women Speak*, Kari Gunter Seymour, ed., vol seven, Sheila-Na-Gig editions, 2021

"Where Fish Dream" *Anthology of Appalachian Writers*, Barbara Kingsolver, ed., vol. 15, Shepherd University, 2023

www.ingramcontent.com/pod-product-compliance
Lightning Source LLC
Chambersburg PA
CBHW032236080426
42735CB00008B/886